Georgetown Elementary School
Indian Prairie School District
Aurora, Illinois

A TRUE BOOK™

Astronaut:
Dr. Mae Jemison
The 100 Year Starship

DR. MAE JEMISON
AND DANA MEACHEN RAU

Children's Press®
An Imprint of Scholastic Inc.
New York Toronto London Auckland Sydney
Mexico City New Delhi Hong Kong
Danbury, Connecticut

Library of Congress Cataloging-in-Publication Data

Jemison, Mae, 1956–
  The 100 year starship / by Dr. Mae Jemison and Dana Meachen Rau.
    pages cm. — (A true book)
  Audience: Age 9–12.
  Audience: Grades 4 to 6.
  Includes bibliographical references and index.
  ISBN 978-0-531-25500-1 (lib. bdg.) — ISBN 978-0-531-24060-1 (pbk.)
  1. Interstellar travel — Juvenile literature. 2. Manned space flight — Juvenile literature. I. Rau, Dana
Meachen, 1971– II. Title. III. Title: One hundred year starship.
  TL793.J46 2013
  629.45 — dc23   2012035761

© 2013 Scholastic Inc.

**Front cover: Child pointing
to the stars
Back cover: Earth**

Find the Truth!

Everything you are about to read is true *except* for one of the sentences on this page.

Which one is **TRUE**?

T or F   Travel to the closest star would take tens of thousands of years with today's chemical fuel rockets.

T or F   Because of weightlessness in space, humans could not survive a trip to another star.

Find the answers in this book.

Contents

1 Giant Leaps in History

What is the 100 Year Starship initiative? 7

2 Journey to the Stars

How do scientists measure interstellar space? 15

3 Designing a Starship

What type of vehicle will we need to travel to interstellar space? 21

THE **BIG** TRUTH!

Powerful Ideas

What types of energy could power a starship? 30

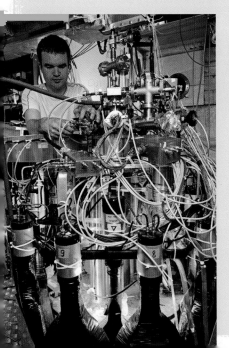

Members of the 100 Year Starship team come from a variety of fields.

4 Living in Interstellar Space

How will humans survive the trip? 33

5 Here and Now

How will planning for a trip to the stars improve life on Earth today? 41

True Statistics 44

Resources 45

Important Words 46

Index 47

About the Authors 48

Scientists have confirmed more than 700 planets outside our solar system.

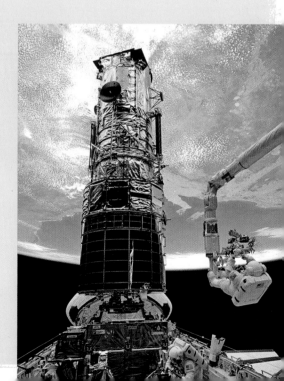

Portuguese explorer Ferdinand Magellan discovered the Strait of Magellan, a shortcut between the Atlantic and Pacific Oceans.

CHAPTER 1

Giant Leaps in History

Throughout history, people have set out on new adventures. Explorers traveled across continents. They settled lands and hunted, farmed, and traded to survive. Over time, people developed new ways to travel across the land, sea, and even the sky. Exploration, invention, and discovery have led to giant leaps in human history. They have taught us a lot about our world. They have helped us improve our lives.

Magellan's crew was the first to sail around the world.

New Technologies

Tools and machines have had giant leaps, too. Long ago, people copied books by hand. Today, we can download and read books on small computers. Horses and steam once powered machines. Today, we use electricity. People once created legends to explain objects and occurrences they did not understand. Today, scientists can use microscopes, telescopes, and other devices to try to solve mysteries surrounding the tiniest objects to the largest ones.

The Large Hadron Collider is a very big device designed to help scientists study the universe's smallest particles.

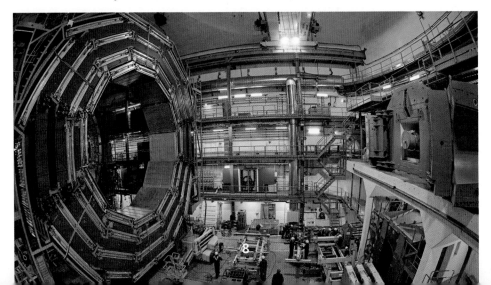

Neil Armstrong can be seen in the reflection on Buzz Aldrin's helmet.

Neil Armstrong took this picture of Edwin "Buzz" Aldrin. The astronauts were the first people to land on the moon.

New **technologies** have helped explorers move beyond Earth into space. Russia, the United States, and China have all sent people into **orbit** around Earth. In 1969, the National Aeronautics and Space Administration (NASA) sent people to land on the moon. NASA and other organizations have also sent **probes** to study the planets. We know a lot about our own solar system and space neighborhood. Many people are curious to explore even farther.

100YSS's plan is not to build an actual ship. It is to explore and create the technologies to make human interstellar flight possible.

The Next Giant Leap

The 100 Year Starship (100YSS) initiative was created to plan the next giant leap in human history. The project will investigate, research, and prepare for humans to travel beyond our solar system to other stars.

Scientists, engineers, teachers, and researchers from around the world gathered in 2011 to consider **interstellar** space travel. The Defense Advanced Research Projects Agency (DARPA), with support from NASA, put out a call for ideas.

Leading the Way

DARPA awarded money to the team with the best plan in 2012. The **proposal** from Dr. Mae Jemison's team won. They will use the money to start 100YSS. Dr. Jemison is a former NASA astronaut. She was the first woman of color in space as a crew member of the space shuttle *Endeavour* in 1992. She has also been an engineer, doctor, businessperson, and professor. Now her job is to lead the 100YSS team.

Jemison spent 190 hours, 30 minutes, and 23 seconds in space.

SETI uses telescopes such as the Arecibo radio telescope to search for life outside our solar system.

100YSS team members include the Dorothy Jemison Foundation for Excellence, Icarus Interstellar, the Search for Extraterrestrial Intelligence (SETI) Institute, schools, museums, and businesses. The experts involved know about space, life sciences, education, and technology. Some members are experts at organizing and running big projects. Dr. Jemison, her team, and the people who come after them will work over the next 100 years to make human travel to other stars possible.

Inclusive and Audacious

Dr. Jemison's proposal was called "An Inclusive, Audacious Journey Transforms Life Here on Earth and Beyond." *Inclusive* means all types of people working together. Scientists, engineers, doctors, businesspeople, writers, and artists from across the globe will work together. *Audacious* means to be bold, think big, and take risks. Interstellar travel takes courage. Hard work and patience are needed to develop new technologies. The *journey* is the starship's trip, but also the planning, experimentation, and imagination that make it possible. 100YSS hopes to change life for the better here on Earth, while aiming for the stars.

Several probes, such as *New Horizons*, have traveled through interplanetary space. But probes have yet to travel to another star.

CHAPTER 2

Journey to the Stars

Our sun is a star. Our solar system is centered on the sun. The sun's gravity holds objects in orbits around it. Planets, asteroids, and comets all travel in paths around this central star. The space within our solar system is called interplanetary space. *Interplanetary* refers to the space between the planets. 100YSS would venture beyond our solar system into interstellar space. This is the space between the stars.

New Horizons will take about nine years to reach its destination.

Space Measurements

It is hard to imagine the large distances of interstellar space. Scientists measure space in a few different ways. They may use astronomical units, called AU. One astronomical unit equals the average distance between Earth and the sun. This is about 93 million miles (150 million kilometers). This unit is often used to describe the distance of a planet from its star.

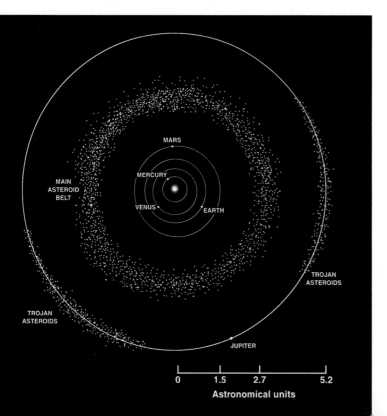

This diagram shows the distances in astronomical units of nearby asteroids and the first five planets from our sun.

 The sun's light takes about eight minutes to reach Earth.

Light travels in waves. These waves move through space at about 186,000 miles per second (300,000 kilometers per second). Scientists use light to measure really large distances. A light-year is the distance light travels in one year, which is more than 6 trillion miles (9.7 trillion km). Scientists may also use an even larger measurement called a parsec. A parsec is about 3.26 light-years. Distances to stars and galaxies can be measured in light-years and parsecs.

Based on what we know about these stars, Alpha Centauri A and B (right) are larger than Proxima Centauri (top). Our sun (left) is shown in the distance, surrounded by a cloud of objects called the Oort cloud.

Choosing a Destination

One reason to explore space is to discover worlds like Earth. With special telescopes, scientists have been looking for and finding **exoplanets** orbiting other stars. Our galaxy has billions of stars, so it will take a long time to find all of these planets. The closest stars to our solar system are the Alpha Centauri-Proxima Centauri triple star system. It is about 4.2 light-years away. Astronomers found a planet orbiting Alpha Centauri B in 2012.

Another nearby star with a planet is Epsilon Eridani. It is 10.5 light-years away. However, neither nearby planet is probably **habitable**. Alpha Centauri B's planet orbits too close to its star. Epsilon Eridani's planet is a lot like our planet Jupiter, which we believe cannot support life as we know it. Kepler is a space telescope looking for Earthlike planets. It has found many candidates for such Earthlike planets in habitable zones around stars. The habitable zone is an area just the right distance from a star. Planets orbiting within this zone are more likely to support life.

Epsilon Eridani's planet is about 3.39 AU from the star.

19

The USS *Enterprise* is a fictional starship made famous by the television show *Star Trek*.

CHAPTER 3

Designing a Starship

The author H. G. Wells wrote a novel in 1901 called *The First Men in the Moon*. Within 70 years, NASA really did send people to the moon. There have been many movies and television shows about spacecraft traveling beyond our solar system. The 100YSS team believes that we are not far from making that dream real, too. It will work to make a starship possible within 100 years.

A starship is a spaceship designed for interstellar travel.

Interstellar Probe Ideas

Some scientists have already designed potential interstellar spacecraft. Project Daedalus in the 1970s looked at the possibility of travel to Barnard's Star, about 6 light-years away. In 2009, Project Icarus began another study of robotic interstellar probes using all the advances of the previous 30 years. 100YSS will take these ideas even further. It will look at human interstellar travel.

Project Daedalus's spacecraft *Daedalus* was never built. But its design provides 100YSS with ideas for interstellar travel.

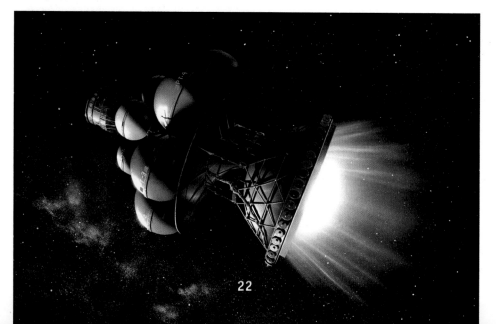

22

Delta II rockets launched Kepler into orbit at about 23,760 miles per hour (38,238 kph).

Getting Started

Space is a **vacuum**. That means there is nothing in space to slow down a spacecraft. An object in a vacuum continues on the same path at the same speed. Chemical rockets **propel** today's spacecraft. These rockets give the craft a big burst of energy at the start of its journey. Then the spacecraft keeps traveling at that speed through space.

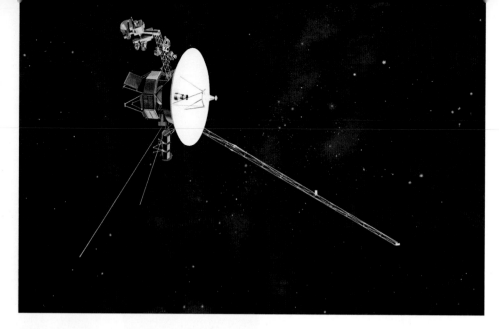

Both *Voyagers 1* and *2* used the gravity of Jupiter to gather speed during their journeys.

Are We There Yet?

NASA launched the probe *Voyager 1* in 1977 on a tour of the solar system and beyond. It is now more than 100 AU from Earth. *Voyager 1* travels at 17,000 miles per hour (27,359 kph). If you compare the trip between Earth and Proxima Centauri, our closest neighboring star, to a trip between California and New York, *Voyager 1* has only traveled about 1 mile (1.6 km). It would take 70,000 years to get to Proxima Centauri!

The *Apollo* missions sped through space at 25,000 miles per hour (40,234 kph). The *Pioneer* missions reached speeds of 110,000 miles per hour (177,028 kph). But even these speeds aren't enough to get us very far very fast. To travel to interstellar space within a lifetime, engineers would have to develop systems to propel a spacecraft at least one-tenth the speed of light. This is about 28,600 miles per second (46,027 km/sec).

It took *Apollo* missions more than three days to reach the moon.

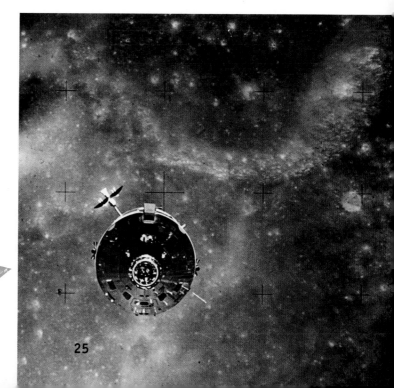

Enough Power

With the chemical fuel rockets we use today, it would take tens of thousands of years to reach the nearest star. So the 100YSS team is looking into new ways to propel spacecraft. It has to decide if a spacecraft needs a short, strong burst at the beginning of the journey, or a slow and continuous push as it travels.

Exploring Possibilities Timeline

1901
Author H. G. Wells publishes *The First Men in the Moon.*

1969
Neil Armstrong and Buzz Aldrin are the first humans to land on the moon.

1973–1978
Project Daedalus studies the possibilities of a starship.

All matter is made up of tiny materials called atoms. Atoms may be a power source for spacecraft. This is called nuclear energy. Nuclear fission is a process that creates energy by breaking atoms apart. Nuclear fusion makes energy by combining atoms. These processes, and others not yet discovered, may be ways to power a starship.

2009
Project Icarus continues the studies of Project Daedalus.

2112
The 100YSS team hopes to have created technologies to make a real starship possible.

2012
Dr. Mae Jemison and her team are awarded a grant to start 100YSS.

Protection from Space

Space is not a friendly place. Engineers will need to design a spacecraft to keep humans protected on a long journey. On Earth, our atmosphere protects us. The atmosphere is the air surrounding our planet. There is no air in space. Temperatures jump from extremely hot in the sun to extremely cold in the shade. Interstellar space is also a very cold place the farther one gets from the sun.

From space, Earth's atmosphere seems to glow blue as it reflects the sun's light.

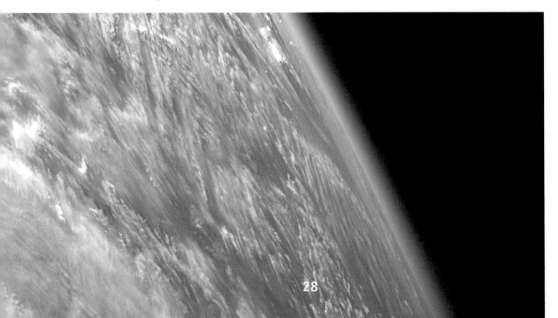

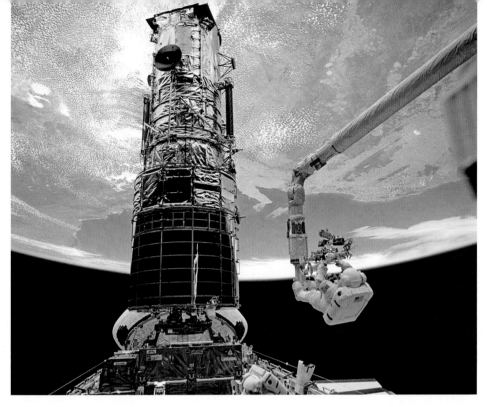

Astronauts and spacecraft need protection from the hazards of space.

The energy flowing out of our sun is called radiation. Some forms of radiation can be harmful. Space is also filled with micrometeoroids. These tiny pieces of space dust can cause a lot of damage to a high-speed spacecraft. The spacecraft will have to be strong to stand up to the harshness of space. It has to be lightweight, too. Then it will need less energy to propel it at high speeds through space.

Powerful Ideas

A starship will need a lot of power to travel to interstellar space. These are some possible sources scientists will consider.

Nuclear fission is used to generate some of the heat and electricity we use on Earth. Some spacecraft already use fission to power instruments on board. But fission can be dangerous, and new methods are needed to make it safer for human use on a starship.

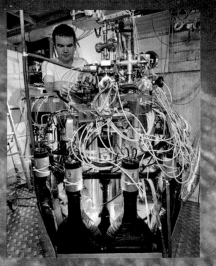

Antimatter is one of the most powerful possible sources of energy known to scientists. But antimatter has only been created in very small amounts in very special laboratories. And it has only existed for very short periods of time. It's not ready for a starship yet.

Nuclear fusion is the same process that the sun uses to create energy. Scientists have experimented with combining atoms in laboratories. More work needs to be done to make a spacecraft engine that can run on nuclear fusion.

More research and imagination will help scientists think of even more "powerful" ideas.

Food on the International Space Station is supplied from Earth.

CHAPTER 4

Living in Interstellar Space

The International Space Station (ISS) orbits Earth. It is "home" to crews of astronauts. These astronauts live, work, eat, and sleep in space for four to six months at a time. Scientists have studied how space affects the astronauts' bodies. On a starship, however, astronauts might be in space for a whole lifetime. The 100YSS team will think about ways for a crew to survive the long trip.

Objects on the ISS are tied down so they don't float around the cabin— including the crew when they sleep!

33

Lots of Questions

What do you need to live on Earth? You need air to breathe, water to drink, and food to eat. On the ISS, the food and water the crew needs is supplied from Earth. **Filters** keep air and water clean. A starship could bring along some supplies. But the ship could fly farther if it could reuse or create **resources** of its own.

Air sampling devices filter the air on the ISS to make sure it is safe.

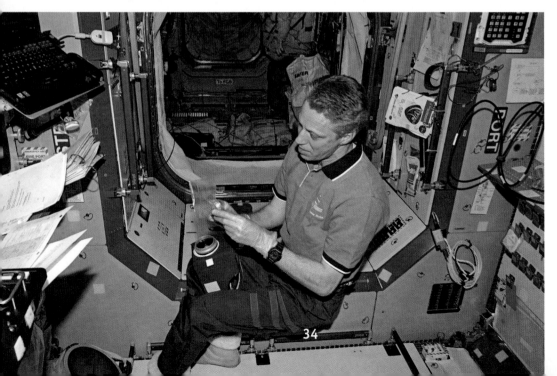

Plants need sun, water, carbon dioxide, and nutrients from the soil to grow. A starship would need these elements for crew members to grow their own food.

The 100YSS team has lots of questions to answer. What will the crew eat? How will the crew keep air and water clean of harmful **toxins**? A starship might have its own garden. The crew could grow fruits, vegetables, and other plants. New systems will make and clean the air and water. Starship designers will also have to think about other daily needs. How will the crew bathe, sleep, throw out trash, and even go to the bathroom?

New technologies could help astronauts navigate through space and even land on exoplanets.

Getting There

The spacecraft will need new technologies for the crew to **navigate** the route through space. It will need computers to collect information. It will need to communicate with Earth. All of these machines will need backup systems in case any break down. The crew will have to know how to fix the machines when needed.

All of the technologies of a starship will also help the crew members when they arrive at their destination. There may not be a source of air or water on an exoplanet. If crew members decide to stay, they will need the tools to survive. The starship will have to provide these necessities.

This artist's illustration shows imagined forms of shelter and transportation. A starship might need to provide these items to crew members who stay on an exoplanet.

Weightlessness

There is no gravity in space. Astronauts feel weightless. It is possible to live in a weightless environment. And floating through the air looks like fun. But too much time in weightlessness makes bones thin and muscles weak. Crew members will have to spend time exercising each day to keep their bodies strong. 100YSS will also look at ways to create the feeling of gravity on a starship to help solve this problem.

Astronauts on the ISS exercise on treadmills and other equipment to stay strong.

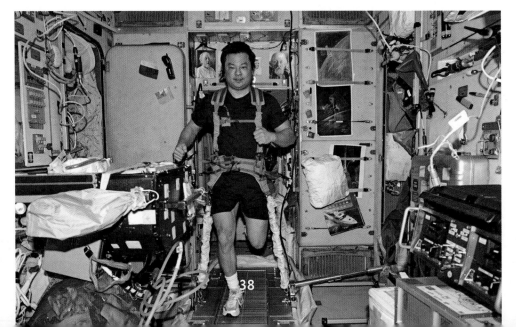

Artificial Gravity

Astronauts orbiting Earth feel weightless because both the spacecraft and its crew are moving, or "falling," through space at the same speed at all times. Outside Earth's orbit, in deep space, crews will be in an environment with very little gravity.

Some starship ideas might include artificial gravity. Artificial gravity can be created with a vehicle that spins. A ship that **accelerates**, or continues to speed up, the entire journey would also create a feeling of weight.

Even before humans travel to interstellar space, life on Earth can be improved by 100YSS research.

CHAPTER 5

Here and Now

The 100YSS team is excited to look toward the future. It imagines a starship that will discover worlds humans have never explored before. New technologies and methods we already have may one day make interstellar travel possible. The inventions, research, and discoveries of the 100YSS team will also help life here on Earth now. We won't have to wait 100 years.

The first space tourist paid $20 million to visit the ISS in 2001.

Solving Earth's Problems

We burn a lot of fuels, such as oil and coal, to create energy on Earth. But those resources will run out someday. As scientists look into ways to power a starship, they will find ways to use that energy on Earth, too. We pollute water and air on Earth. If researchers find new ways to clean them for a starship, we can use what they've learned to help clean Earth's air and water.

Cars and other vehicles run on gasoline, which is made from oil.

Starships might include greenhouses or space gardens to grow food.

We'll learn more about our bodies as we study the effect of space on astronauts. This may help prevent diseases such as bone loss. Perhaps we'll solve hunger problems by finding new ways to grow crops. We'll create new materials and communication methods. The ways a starship will help Earth are endless. Dr. Mae Jemison and the 100YSS team dream big. The giant leap into interstellar space will be a giant leap for everyone on Earth, too. ⭐

True Statistics

Leader of the 100YSS team: Dr. Mae Jemison

Members of the 100YSS team include: Alires Almon; Richard Obousy, PhD; Marianne Caponnetto; and Andreas Tziolas, PhD

Methods to measure distance in space: Light-years, astronomical units, and parsecs

Closest star: Proxima Centauri, at 4.2 light-years away

Closest star with an exoplanet: Alpha Centauri B, at 4.4 light-years away

Possible starship power sources: Nuclear fission, nuclear fusion, and antimatter

Did you find the truth?

T Travel to the closest star would take tens of thousands of years with today's chemical fuel rockets.

F Because of weightlessness in space, humans could not survive a trip to another star.

Resources

Books

Bortz, Alfred B. *Seven Wonders of Space Technology*. Minneapolis: Twenty-First Century Books, 2011.

Miller, Gary. *The Outer Limits: The Future of Space Exploration*. Pleasantville, NY: Gareth Stevens Publishing, 2010.

Parker, Steve. *Future Transport In Space*. New York: Marshall Cavendish Benchmark, 2012.

Sparrow, Giles. *Space Exploration*. Mankato, MN: Smart Apple Media, 2012.

Visit the 100 Year Starship Web site at *100YSS.org* for more information on the challenges of travel to another star and ideas on how to solve them. You can also learn about the people who are trying to make the dream a reality!

Visit this Scholastic Web site for more information on 100 Year Starship:
★ www.factsfornow.scholastic.com
Enter the keywords **100 Year Starship**

Important Words

accelerates (ak-SEL-uh-rayts) — gets faster and faster

exoplanets (EKS-oh-plan-its) — planets that are outside our solar system

filters (FIL-turz) — devices that clean liquids or gases as they pass through

habitable (HAB-i-tuh-buhl) — safe to live on

interstellar (in-tur-STEL-ur) — part of the space between stars

navigate (NAV-i-gate) — to find where you are and where you need to go when you travel in a ship, an aircraft, or other vehicle

orbit (OR-bit) — a curved path around a planet or star

probes (PROHBZ) — devices used to explore space

propel (pruh-PEL) — to push something forward

proposal (pruh-POZE-uhl) — an official written suggestion for a course of action

resources (REE-sors-iz) — things that are of value or use

technologies (tek-NAH-luh-jeez) — practical devices and applications of scientific and engineering knowledge

toxins (TOKS-inz) — poisonous substances

vacuum (VAK-yoom) — a space that is empty of gas, dust, or other matter

Index

Page numbers in **bold** indicate illustrations.

air, 28, **34**, 35, 37, 42
antimatter, **31**
Apollo missions, **9**, **25**, **26**
astronauts, **9**, **11**, **29**, **32**, 33, **36**, **38**, 39, 43
atoms, 27, 31

communication, 36, 43

Defense Advanced Research Projects Agency (DARPA), 10, 11

Earth, 9, 13, 16, **17**, **28**, **30**, **32**, 33, 34, 36, **40**, 41, **42**, 43
Endeavour (space shuttle), **11**
exercise, **38**
exoplanets, 18, **19**, **36**, **37**
exploration, **6**, 7, **9**

fission, 27, **30**
food, **32**, 34, **35**, **43**
fusion, 27, 31

grants, 11, 27
gravity, 15, **24**, 38, 39

habitable zones, 19

International Space Station (ISS), **32**, 33, **34**, **38**, 41
interplanetary space, **14**, 15
interstellar space, 10, 13, 15, 16, 21, **22**, 25, 28, 30, 41

Jemison, Mae, **11**, 12, 13, 27, 43

measurements, **16**–17
moon, **9**, 21, **25**, **26**

National Aeronautics and Space Administration (NASA), 9, 10, 11, 21, 24
navigation, **36**
nuclear energy, 27, **30**, 31

Pioneer missions, 25
pollution, 35, 42
probes, 9, **14**, 15, **22**, **24**
Project Daedalus, **22**, 26, 27
Project Icarus, 22, 27
proposal, 11, 13
propulsion, **23**, 25, 26–27, 29, 30, 31, **39**
Proxima Centauri, **18**, 24

rockets, **23**, 26

solar system, 9, 15, 18, 24
speed, **17**, 23, **24**–25, 29, 39
stars, **14**, 15, 16, 17, **18**–**19**, 22, 24, 26
starships, 13, **20**, 21, 26, 27, 30, 33, 34, 35, **37**, 38, **39**, 41, 42, **43**
sun, 15, **16**, **17**, **18**, **28**, 29, **30**, **31**, **35**

technologies, **8**–**9**, **10**, 12, 13, 27, **36**–37, 41
telescopes, 8, **12**, 18, 19
temperatures, 28

vacuums, 23
Voyager probes, **24**

water, 34, **35**, 37, 42

About the Authors

Dr. Mae Jemison is leading 100 Year Starship (100YSS). This is a new initiative to make human space travel to another star possible within the next 100 years. Dr. J is a medical doctor, engineer, and entrepreneur, or businessperson. She was a NASA astronaut and flew aboard the space shuttle *Endeavour* in 1992. She was the world's first woman of color in space. Dr. J was a college professor, author, and started several businesses. She also works to get more students involved in science. She started an international science camp for students called The Earth We Share. Dr. J enjoys dancing, gardening, and art. She lives in Houston and loves cats!

Dana Meachen Rau is the author of more than 300 books for children. A graduate of Trinity College in Hartford, Connecticut, she has written fiction and nonfiction titles, including early readers and books on science, history, cooking, and many other topics that interest her. Dana lives with her family in Burlington, Connecticut.

PHOTOGRAPHS © 2013: AP Images/North Wind Picture Archives: 6; Corbis Images/Topic Photo Agency: cover; Ctein/(http://ctein.com): 5 top, 10; Getty Images: 20 (CBS Photo Archive), 8 (Lionel Flusin/Gamma-Rapho); NASA: 19, 32 (European Space Agency), back cover (Goddard Space Flight Center), 5 bottom, 29 (Hubble Space Telescope Collection), 14 (Johns Hopkins University Applied Physics Laboratory), 25 (Johnson Space Center), 24 (JPL), 28 (JPL/UCSD/JSC), 23 (Kim Shiflett), 16 (Lunar and Planetary Institute), 30 background, 31 background (Solar and Heliospheric Observatory), 3, 9, 11, 26, 34, 38, 44; Photo Researchers: 13 (Chris Butler), 37, 43 (Christian Darkin), 4, 12, 31 foreground (David Parker), 36 (Detlev van Ravenswaay), 18 (Julian Baum), 30 foreground (Martin Bond), 40 (Richard Bizley), 22, 27, 39 (Shigemi Numazawa); Shutterstock, Inc.: 42 (chung king), 35 (Federico Rostagno), 17 (Kovnir Andrii).